THIS BOOK IS TOAST

Contributions from

Joanna Lumley

Jane Asher

Jeremy Robson

Photography Maria Andrews

Food stylist Karol Gladki

A percentage of the profits go to Spread a Smile

THIS BOOK IS TOAST

Tempting Recipes for Toppings on Toast

Heidi Nathan

Amusing Musings by Dame Maureen Lipman

Best Books and Films

Published in 2021
by Best Books and Films
an imprint of
Psychology News Press
92a Hoxton Street
London N1 6LP

dcpsychologynews@gmail.com

Copyright © Heidi Nathan and Dame Maureen Lipman 2021

Heidi Nathan and Dame Maureen Lipman have asserted their rights
under the Copyright, Patents and Designs Act 1988
to be identified as the author of the work.

The publishers thank Joanna Lumley, Jane Asher and Jeremy Robson
for permission to use their material.

Typeset by Keyboard Services, Luton, Beds.
Printed by Spauda in Lithuania.
Second impression 2021.

All rights reserved. No part of this publication may be reproduced, stored in a retrieval system or transmitted, in any form or by any means, without the publisher's prior permission in writing.

This book is sold subject to the condition that it shall not, by way of trade or otherwise, be lent, resold, hired out or otherwise circulated without the publisher's prior consent in any form of binding or cover other than that in which it is published and without a similar condition, including this condition, being imposed on the subsequent purchaser.

Every reasonable effort has been made to trace copyright holders of material reproduced in this book, but if any have been inadvertently overlooked the publisher would be glad to hear from them.

ISBN 978-0-907-63313-6

Contents

Foreword by Maureen Lipman 2

A Few Crumbs by Heidi Nathan 4

Toast has always been pretty central to my life by Joanna Lumley 8

What Came First, the Toast or the Bread? 10

Chapter One 14
    Pickled Vegetables and Perfect Sauces 14

Two Cautionary Tales by Jeremy Robson 24

Chapter Two 26
    Everything Tastes Better with Melted Cheese 26

Chapter Three 44
    Loaded with Vegetables 44

Slice and Assemble 46

Here are some easy and totally delicious dips that work brilliantly served with toasted pita or any thinly toasted bread 70

Chapter Four 76
    Add Some Protein 76

Loafing by Maureen Lipman 96

Chapter Five 98
    Sweet Things 98

The Last Slice in the Rack by Maureen Lipman 112

The Last Word by Heidi Nathan 115

FOREWORD

Maureen Lipman

There is a famous comic story in my family concerning my late and much missed muse and mother Zelma. She was complaining, mildly, about arthritic pain in her hands. Ever the know-it-all, doctor manqué, I advised her to withdraw wheat from her diet for a week and see if it made any difference.

'Wheat?' she asked me with astonished intonation, 'I don't eat wheat. Why would I eat wheat?' It was as if I had suggested she gave up sucking wasps for a week.

'Well, bread,' I said emphatically, 'just don't eat any bread for a week, that's all.'

'Me? Bread? I hardly eat any bread,' she said smugly, adding, 'I don't even buy bread these days. I don't even have a bread-bin.'

There was no more for me to say but I could see her mind working on the subject and in the uncharacteristic silence that followed she looked sideways up at me and asked, doubtfully:

'Is toast bread?'

The point of the story, aside from illustrating just how much comic material I lost when I lost my beloved mother, was that in her mind toast was a stable. Like aspirin and salt and dried fruit soaking in a basin it was something she took for granted as a necessity. I suspect that as usual with Zelma's little apogees, there was a profound truth in there.

That truth being that toasted bread and butter is the ultimate comfort food. It means, home from school on dark winter evenings with reddened hands and visible breath on your lips. It means Sunday morning toast soldiers arranged in a ring around a perfectly boiled egg, with the top cut off. It means late mornings after a party night, with nothing in the student fridge but half an onion, some pickled beetroot and the bottom of a jar of strawberry jam. It means 'tea' or what you southerners call 'dinner,' of Spaghetti Hoops on soggy white bread toast or beans on one slice and fried egg on the other, in the warmth of your own kitchen, at one a.m. after a night of Chicken à La Crème at some long drawn out and ultimately empty-handed, awards ceremony.

It means *The Famous Five* holding out skewered slices in front of a roaring but containable camp fire and secret midnight kitchen raids at draughty boarding schools to plot important village detective work. It conjures recuperation from childhood disease and first tastes after bilious attacks or minor operations. It means arguments about cold or heated up sardines on top of your toast or whether it is a crime to feed your dog the crusts of your toast under the table or to dip them surreptitiously in your tea to protect your bridgework.

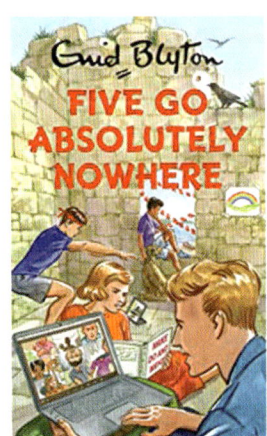

'Bread and water can so easily be tea and toast' was famously written on a tea towel and in the pages of *Punch* magazine in 1852 where a man cried, 'No bread? Then bring me toast!'

Or when the wonderfully droll Edward Lear wrote:

> There was an old man of the coast
> Who placidly sat on a post;
> But when it was cold,
> He relinquished his hold
> And called for some hot buttered toast.

You need a magnifying glass to spot the toast.

So, Ladies and Gentlemen, gender fluid and binaries, children and Master chefs, may I ask you to raise your cups, glasses, spirits, and Ribena's as I propose a Toast?

To … er … TOAST!

A FEW CRUMBS

Heidi Nathan

I love food and cooking for friends and family is one of my greatest pleasures. I live on my own, so cuisine for one is a curious business. People often ask me if I cook my signature dishes, baked lamb, salt beef, chicken soup etc for myself – and the answer is yes, sometimes I do. Making a soup or stew and freezing portions is an absolute given as I always cook as though I'm catering for ten.

But in the Groundhog days (this book has been developed during COVID 19), we find ourselves in these days – it has become my guilt trip to just stick whatever is left in the fridge on a slice of hot buttered toast. At the expense of my BMI, this, shamefully, has become primarily how I eat.

I was having a lockdown walk with my neighbour and friend Maureen Lipman … sorry, Dame Maureen Lipman, and she was prising out of me, as only she can, my appalling TV-watching habits of Real Housewives of anywhere in the world and other equally such quality viewing. We paused for a soya Cappuccino from a van, and she fixed me with a beady, bespectacled eye over the top of a pleated silk mask plus Perspex visor and said: 'Oh, Heidi, do YOU need a project?'

I have a job I love, working for a charity that works to improve the lives of seriously and terminally ill children in hospital. I'm always busy. I walk, I read, I phone my mother in South Africa daily (with not much to say these days), I do the odd jigsaw, etc. and I watch questionable television.

I felt my face taking on a tinge of embarrassment – which she jumped on like the clever ferret she is:

'What about that book you mentioned months ago, about things to have on toast?' she asked. 'Have you done anything about it?'

'Er?'

'You haven't have you?'

'Well, I've thought about it, once or twice.'

'Right. Well, get on with it. I've got a good title for you.'

'What?'

'I'll tell you when you've done the recipes.'

There was no escape. I trudged off in my direction and she in hers. The die was cast. I had to apply the seat of my trousers to the seat of a chair and start. Very quickly it became an obsession and soon the long nights of insomnia were filled with fillings. Instead of watching another mindless television programme I was dusting platters and arranging Ciabatta prettily on Arugula leaves.

What has emerged is not necessarily a recipe or a cook book, but more a compilation of ideas and suggestions of ingredients that look and taste good on toast. Most of the recipes have a simple store-bought option and some require a bit of cooking. But all are favourites that will inspire you to make not just a piece of toast, but a whole meal, often on wholemeal.

I have also asked some of my nearest and dearest to give me some of their favourite things to put on toast and Maureen has badgered the great and the near great into doing the same.

Most of the recipes have a bread recommendation, but in most cases it's just a suggestion. There are so many varieties available, so please experiment. If Roast on Toast is your thing then slam on the wholegrain mustard and go for it.

Jane Asher literally 'egging her pudding'

FRIED EGGS ON TOAST

This must be one of the quickest cakes in the book if you use a ready-made sponge and an aerosol of cream – it's very silly, but, I think, enormous fun.

1 rectangular flat sponge
tin of half peaches
whipped cream or aerosol cream

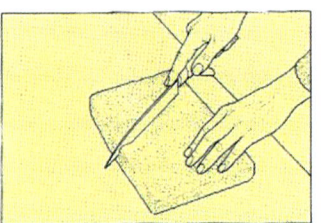

1 *Cut sponge in half to look like two pieces of toast.*

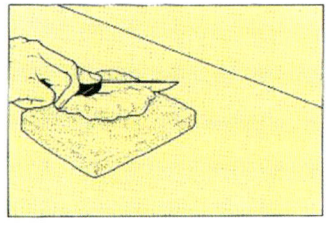

2 *Spread or spray cream onto sponge cakes.*

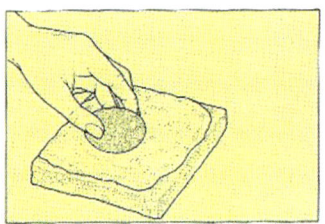

3 *Press peach halves into cream.*

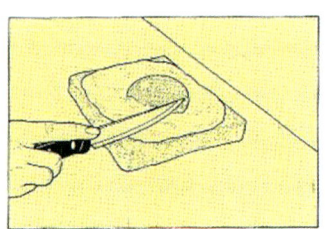

4 *Pull cream up around peaches with a knife.*

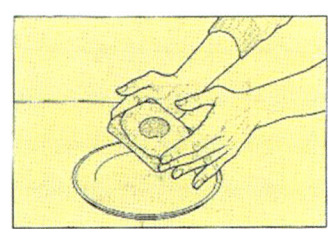

5 *Put on a plate.*

6 *Add a knife and fork if desired for fun.*

See opposite.

TOAST HAS ALWAYS BEEN PRETTY CENTRAL TO MY LIFE

Joanna Lumley

On it I put:

Home-made marmalade, quite sour, quite chunky.

Marmite: and sometimes peanut butter on top of the Marmite, with watercress squashed onto the top of that.

Baked beans, pronounced baked beings, for no reason other than to get an easy laugh.

Butter to melt through, and then salt, pepper and chopped up herbs like mint, basil and parsley with a dollop of mayonnaise.

Raspberry jam, with a few fresh raspberries and a blob of clotted cream.

Mashed bananas, with brown sugar and sultanas sprinkled over.

Cream cheese, sunflower seed hearts with black pepper and sea salt.

Tomatoes squashed in a pan with butter until they are shapeless, then blobbed onto Marmite toast.

Grated extra strong Cheddar cheese sprinkled thickly onto toast already spread with English mustard, and then browned under the grill.

WHAT CAME FIRST, THE TOAST OR THE BREAD?

Toast scholars wouldn't be scholars if they didn't have academic differences. Some say Toast was actually created long before bread. Individual pieces were cooked over open flames for centuries before Isaac Load, the Earl of Bread (?) hit upon the idea of forming toast dough into logs, toasting it, then slicing the finished product. (Seems unlikely to me.)

Others say it's likely that people were making flat-breads 30,000 years ago. There is early archaeological evidence that grain was ground to produce flour, made into a dough, then baked into a flatbread over an open fire.

Before the development of the electric toaster, hand sliced bread had to be toasted on a long metal fork or in a metal frame held over a fire, or on a gas stove. Simple utensils for toasting bread over open flames appeared in the early 19th century.

Charred crumbs made by Natufian hunter-gatherers from wild wheat, wild barley and plant roots between 14,600 and 11,600 years ago have been found at the archaeological site of Shubayqa 1 in the Black Desert in Jordan, predating the earliest known making of bread from cultivated wheat by thousands of years.

Bread as we know it today was probably invented in ancient Egypt. The Egyptians learned that if they left dough sitting out for a while, it would rise. When baked, the bread would retain its risen shape. The closed oven was invented in Egypt for the baking of leavened breads by 3000 BC, and the workers who built the famous pyramids were often paid partially with bread. The bread-maker was invented in (?) for locked-down middle class 'foodies' to show off their artisan plaiting and graining skills.

Back in Pharoanic days, there was just one problem: left out in the desert heat for long periods of time, bread would go hard and become difficult to chew. It's likely that toast originated as a way to preserve bread; used to prolong its life and prevent mould from growing on.

Perhaps one house-proud Egyptian tidying up the cooking area, threw away some bread on the simmering coals – glancing sideways as she did it because it is bad karma in the Middle East to throw away bread – and Lo!

> 'By the gleam in my eye and the scarab in your beard
> Something quite toasty hath appeared.'

'Hey, Potiphar,' she called out in cool but colloquial Aramaic, 'get this! Hot crispy bread! Slap a bit of Egyptian goose fat on this and I think we may have a nice little earner.'

'And don't tell the pesky Romans!' she may have added.

But here's what the Romans did do for us? Surely, they explained to us patiently claiming the knowledge as their own, not the conquered Egyptian's that toasting bread was a way of preserving its freshness and palatability.

It is, of course, unlikely they referred to it as toast. The word 'toast' is thought to have come from the Latin 'tostum', to scorch or burn, but it's a fairly modern word. (How can it be both modern and Latin?)

Patriotic Brits claim toasting was invented at the Battle of Hastings in 1066 when bread became wet and needed to be dried on shields next to the bonfire. Resulting in what they hadn't expected, crispy and tasty hot bread!

At any rate, the first breads were probably toasted by laying them in front of the fire on a hot stone or a piece of pyramid. Later, simple devices were created to toast bread in the fire, using wire frames or even sticks to cook the toast more evenly.

Bread was an early 'fast food' for the masses. It could sustain armies, save explorers, pad out school dinners and be a staple for the poor. Fresh bread was, and still is, appreciated for its flavour, smell, colour quality, visual appearance and texture. Fans

'At least we don't have to eat Matza'

of P.G. Wodehouse know that in the Drones Club the young idle rich form bread into pellets and throw it at each other.

The how to sell your house at the drop of a hat say that the best way to sell your property is to heat bread in the oven before the potential buyer rings the doorbell. What could be sexier than seeing the traditional French bread poking out of a linen shopping bag across the Place du Montmartre.

But humankind needs progress and is essentially as lazy as a three-toed sloth on a service berry tree. The first electric toaster was invented in 1893 by Scotsman Alan McMasters, but it wasn't very popular. The iron wiring would often melt, creating a regular and irritating fire hazard chez McMasters.

Toasters got increasingly thinner and blended into the late 20th century kitchen neatly, until the tide turned as tides tend to do and bulky alloy mock art deco ones emerged to remove most of your serving up space.

Some of these toasters look like science fiction creations.

Meanwhile, an invention was in the works that would make grabbing some toast in the morning even easier: pre-sliced bread.

The much-derided re-sliced bread helped to further popularize toast and the toaster, because it was easy to grab a few uniformly cut slices, pop them under the grill or in the toaster, and have breakfast a few minutes later. And the rest, as they say, is Yeastory … sorry about that.

Wikipedia defines toast as:

> Toast is bread which has been grilled until hot and crispy. A toaster, grill or open fire is used. Toasted bread is both darker in colour and crunchier than normal bread. Toast can be eaten with a range of condiments spread on the surface, such as butter, jam, honey, and cheese to make cheese on toast, though these are optional as some people prefer their toast without condiments (dry toast).
>
> Toast can also be used to make 'toasties', where a filling is compressed and heated between two slices of buttered bread in a toastie maker. Popular fillings include cheese, jam, peanut butter and chocolate spread.
>
> Before the invention of modern cooking appliances such as toasters and grills, bread has been produced in ovens for millennia. Toast can be made in the same oven.

Although we think its easy to produce the perfect piece of toast, that couldn't be further from the truth. Indeed, it can be debated, what is perfect? And how do you achieve perfection?

Delia Smith has her own inimitable method for making the perfect piece of toast, not in a toaster, but in the oven:

Her definitive recipe for perfect toast is as follows:

> *To begin with, I am not a disciple of automatic toasters. The ones I've experienced all seem to be a bit hit and miss, and if you're rather inept at slicing*

bread (like me), then they're not very helpful at all because if the bread is slightly wonky; a) it probably won't go in the toaster at all, and, b) if it does, one bit ends up not being toasted at all while the other bit is giving off nasty black smoke signals!

For toast, cut the bread into slices about 1cm thickness. The crusts can be on or off, depending on how you like them. Pre-heat the grill for at least 10 minutes before making the toast, turning it to its highest setting. Place the bread on the grill rack and position the tray 10cm from the heat source. Allow the bread to toast on both sides to your own preferred degree of pale or dark golden brown.

While that's happening, keep an eye on it and don't wander far away. When the toast is done, remove it immediately to a toast rack. Why a toast rack? Because they are a brilliant invention. Freshly made toast contains steam, and if you place it in a vertical position, in which the air is allowed to circulate, the steam escapes and the toast becomes crisp and crunchy. Putting it straight on to a plate means the steam is trapped underneath, making it damp and soggy. If you don't possess a toast rack, you really ought to invest in a modest one. Failing that, stand your toast up against a jar or something similar for about 1 minute before serving.

Always eat toast as soon as possible after that, and never make it ahead of time. Never ever wrap it in a napkin or cover it), because the steam gets trapped and the toast goes soggy. Always use good bread, because the better the bread the better the toast. It is also preferable if the bread is a couple of days old.

Ah, toast. 'How do we love thee. Let me count the ways.' We love you slathered in butter, oozing with cheese, or layered with our favourite topping. Be it morning's first bite or the last thing we eat at night. Versatile and lending itself to endless possibilities, the humble slice presents an opportunity for easy innovation and good old-fashioned comfort. Whatever your fancy or filling, here's how to turn toast into your favourite meal.

CHAPTER ONE

Pickled Vegetables and Perfect Sauces

Convenience stores are full of mass-produced jars of pickled vegetables and sauces. They certainly are convenient and some are delicious, but making your own is honestly not that scary.

Having an array of customised pickles and sauces in your fridge, means you can create mouth-watering dishes with ease. Frankly it's also a cracking way to get you compliments on your condiments.

Pickled vegetables are made simply using a hot sweet, sour or spicy brine to marinate the vegetables, and in just a couple days (and in some cases hours) your quick and easy pickled vegetables are ready to enjoy.

Here are some easy recipes for pickled vegetables and sauces and the best thing is, they really don't require you to have held a MasterChef trophy on high! I have used them liberally in the coming pages.

Pickled Cabbage
Pickled Red Onions
Sweet and Spicy Cucumbers
Mango Chutney
Tahini Dressing
Peri-Peri Sauce
Pesto
Labneh
Tomato Sauce

Sweet and Spicy Cucumbers

2 medium or 5-6 small cucumbers

1 cup water

1 cup white vinegar

½ cup granulated sugar

1 tablespoon coarse salt

2 teaspoons black peppercorns

2 teaspoons whole yellow mustard seed

2 bay leaves

Prepare the cucumber, either leave them whole, or slice into spears or rounds.

Pack tightly into a jar pickling or mason jar.

Combine the water, vinegar, sugar, salt, peppercorns, bay leaves and mustard seeds in a pot and bring to the boil.

Reduce the heat and simmer until the sugar has dissolved.

Remove from the heat and allow to cool for a few minutes, then pour over the cucumbers (double the pickling liquid if necessary, it must fill the jar and cover the cucumbers).

Let the cucumbers and vinegar mixture cool completely and then refrigerate.

Store in the fridge for up to two weeks.

Pickled Cabbage

½ cabbage shredded or sliced

(Red or white cabbage)

1 onion finely diced

2 tablespoons chopped dill

1 cup boiling water

½ cup white vinegar

1 heaped teaspoon salt

1 heaped teaspoon sugar

½ teaspoon caraway seeds

Thinly slice/shred the cabbage into strips and place into a bowl.

Finely dice the onion and chop the dill, mix with the cabbage.

Add the vinegar, salt and sugar to the boiling water and stir until salt and sugar dissolves.

Pour over the cabbage and mix thoroughly.

Allow to sit for at least 30 minutes, but best to be left overnight. Keep it refrigerated.

Pickled Red Onions

1 medium red onion
½ cup white wine vinegar
2 teaspoons granulated sugar
½ teaspoon coarse salt
¼ teaspoon peppercorns

Peel the onion, cut it in half lengthwise and slice thinly.
Pack the slices tightly into canning jar or glass bottle with a lid.
Put the remaining ingredients into a small saucepan and place it over high heat.
Bring the mixture to a boil and simmer for a few minutes until the sugar and salt has dissolved.
Remove from the heat.
If your container isn't heatproof – such as a canning jar – let the brine cool slightly and then pour over the onion.
Leave to cool before putting the lid on the container and then refrigerate.
Keep in the fridge and use within two weeks.

Mango Chutney

2 mangoes (or apples or pears)
½ an onion
1 clove garlic
¼ cup maple syrup or honey
¼ cup red wine vinegar
salt and pepper to taste
¼ teaspoon each of peppercorns, cumin seeds and Nigella seeds
2 cardamon pods

Peel and dice the mangoes, onion and garlic.
n a heavy bottom pan, combine all the ingredients.
Let the ingredients simmer for about 7-10 minutes, stirring often.
Then remove from heat and let cool slightly. It will thicken as it cools.

Labneh

This is great for spreading on savoury or sweet dishes.

1kg natural yogurt
1 teaspoon salt
Muslin cheesecloth and string

Line a large colander with a cheesecloth.
Stir salt into the yogurt, and pour the into the cheesecloth.
Bring the sides together and tie well.
Set the colander in a bowl to catch the liquid that drains off.
Leave to drain for 24 hours.
After draining, transfer the cheese into a bowl or a glass storage jar.
Store covered in the refrigerator for up to two weeks.

Tahini Dressing

1/3 cup Tahini
1 medium lemon, juiced
1-2 tablespoon maple syrup
1 pinch coarse salt
1 clove minced garlic
3-6 tablespoon of water

Whisk together all ingredients in a mixing bowl.
Add water slowly until the dressing is creamy and pourable.
The mixture may seize up and thicken at first, but continue adding water a little at a time and whisking until creamy and smooth.
Can be stored in an air-tight container in the fridge for about 5 days.

Peri-Peri Sauce

This is a must have South African hot sauce and can be used to spice up almost anything!
Try it with the chicken livers and Prego Rolls later in the book.

2 red onions peeled and chopped
1 garlic clove peeled and chopped
1 cup Bird's Eye chillies
2 red peppers, seeds removed and roughly chopped
3 ripe tomatoes, skins removed and roughly chopped
4 tablespoons olive oil
Juice and zest of 3 lemons
1/3 cup red wine vinegar
2 tablespoons sugar
1 tablespoon salt
1 teaspoon black pepper
2 bay leaves
1 tablespoon dried Oregano
1 tablespoon smoked Paprika

Combine all the ingredients in the bowl of a food processor or blender and mix until all the ingredients are finely chopped.
Add a few spoons of water to the mixture if it's not a saucy consistency.
Transfer to a saucepan over medium heat and simmer for 20 minutes, stirring every few minutes to prevent the sauce from burning.
After 20 minutes, check the seasoning and adjust.
The sauce should be well balanced with a good kick of spice and sourness from the lemon and vinegar.
Add extra chilli's if you like things extra hot and spicy.
Pour into jars or bottles and keep in the refrigerator for up to 2 weeks.

Pesto

50g pine nuts
80g basil
50g parmesan
150ml olive oil
2 garlic cloves

Heat a small frying pan over a low heat.
Cook the pine nuts until golden, shaking occasionally.
Put into a food processor with the basil, Parmesan, olive oil and garlic cloves.
Blend until smooth, then season to taste.

Tomato Sauce

2 tablespoons extra virgin olive oil
1 onion, finely chopped
1 small carrot, finely chopped
1 small stalk of celery, finely chopped
2 tablespoons chopped fresh parsley
1 clove garlic, minced
½ teaspoon dried mixed Italian herbs
1 can chopped tomatoes
1 teaspoon tomato paste
Salt and black pepper

Heat olive oil in a large skillet on medium heat.
Add the finely chopped onion, garlic, carrot, celery and parsley and stir.
Cook for about 5-7 minutes until the onions are translucent.
Add the tomatoes, tomato paste, herbs, salt and pepper.
Reduce the heat to low and simmer uncovered for about 15 minutes until the sauce thickens.
Either use chunky or purée for smooth sauce in a blender or with an immersion blender,
to give it a smooth consistency.

Easy option:
Use tinned tomatoes, flavoured with salt, pepper and dried mixed Italian herbs.
Simmer for about 15 minutes to combine the flavours, then cool.
Pour into jars or bottles and keep in the refrigerator for up to 2 weeks.

Toast Lines
Two Cautionary Tales

by Jeremy Robson

Oh Marie!

If only Marie Antoinette
in her finery had kept
her head and not
told the hungry throng
to eat cake but
toast instead,
it might have been
a different story….
and far less gory.

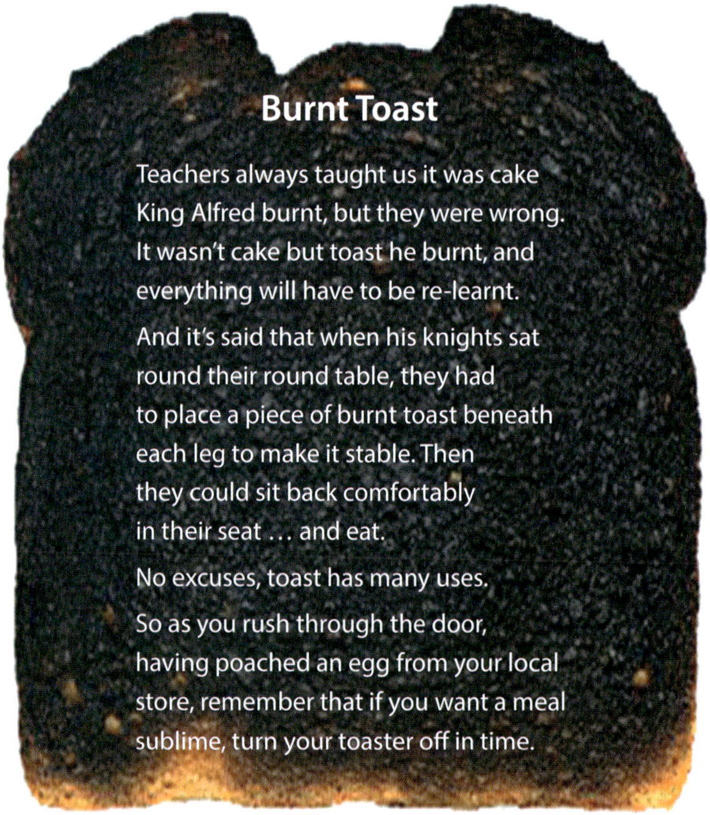

Burnt Toast

Teachers always taught us it was cake
King Alfred burnt, but they were wrong.
It wasn't cake but toast he burnt, and
everything will have to be re-learnt.

And it's said that when his knights sat
round their round table, they had
to place a piece of burnt toast beneath
each leg to make it stable. Then
they could sit back comfortably
in their seat … and eat.

No excuses, toast has many uses.

So as you rush through the door,
having poached an egg from your local
store, remember that if you want a meal
sublime, turn your toaster off in time.

Every animal loves toast

CHAPTER TWO

Everything Tastes Better with Melted Cheese

Breakfast, lunch, dinner or a midnight snack – everything tastes better with melted cheese. You can take the most boring of ingredients, add cheese and melt, and somehow the outcome is always delicious. We all need a bit of comfort food every now and again. I challenge anyone not to agree that a toasted cheese doesn't make the perfect comfort food.

Even if you just start with a piece of toast, add your favourite cheese put it under the grill for a minute or two, you already have a great snack. There are a million meals to make, here are just a few. All have minimal ingredients and are easy to make. Toasted sandwiches can be grilled open-faced under the grill, toasted to perfection in a toasted sandwich maker or made in a heavy skillet on a stove top.

The Best Cheeses for toasted sandwiches:
Brie, Mozzarella, Gruyère, Provolone, Havarti, Cheddar, Gouda, Monterey.

Ultimate Simple Toasted Cheese
Caramelized Onion
Herbed Onion and Parmesan
Roasted Vegetables
Asparagus and Cheese baguette
Leeks and Cheese
Courgette, Pea and Cheese Omelette
Artichoke Hearts and Parmesan
Buffalo Mozzarella and Olives
Mushrooms and Fresh Herbs

Ultimate Toasted Cheese and Tomato

1 teaspoon wholegrain mustard

1 tablespoon mayonnaise

2 handfuls grated cheese such as Cheddar or Gouda
(but the mayonnaise makes it a bit moister so you could
easily use hard cheese such as Parmesan or Manchego)

Sliced tomato

Salt and Pepper

2 slices of toast

Fresh herbs, such as basil or Arugula

Set the oven to Grill

Combine cheese, mustard and mayonnaise and add a pinch of salt and pepper

Place your toast on a baking tray lined with foil or baking paper and completely cover with the cheese mixture.

Arrange the slices of tomato on top of the cheese mixture and place under the grill for 5 minutes or until the cheese is melted and bubbling with golden brown patches.

Make sure you look closely after 5 minutes to make sure they don't burn.

Serve with fresh herbs.

Caramelized Onion with Balsamic Vinegar

2 red onions, sliced

1 tablespoon butter

½ teaspoon salt

¼ teaspoon ground pepper

3 tablespoons balsamic vinegar

Gruyère cheese

Sauté sliced onions in a pan with butter for around 10 minutes until they are soft and translucent., stirring throughout.

Add balsamic vinegar, salt and pepper, stir and sauté for 2-3 minutes until vinegar has soaked into onions.

Remove from the heat

While the onion is cooking, toast your bread and grate your cheese.

Layer the onions onto the toast followed by the cheese.

In a pre-heated the oven at 200C, place the toast onto a baking tray and grill for 2-3 minutes until the cheese has melted.

Add some fresh Rocket just before serving.

Roasted Vegetables

You can use any left-over vegetables or make your fresh.

½ red pepper
½ yellow pepper
½ courgette
½ small onion (white or red)
½ tin of chopped tomatoes
1 tablespoon olive oil
Salt and black pepper
1 teaspoon dried mixed herbs
Pinch red pepper flakes (optional)
Other vegetable options: broccoli, cauliflower
Grated Cheddar cheese

Prepare your vegetables, keeping them roughly the same size for even cooking.
Place onto a rimmed baking sheet and drizzle with olive oil.
Add salt, pepper and mixed herbs and toss to combine.
Bake for 20-25 minutes in an oven pre-heated to 200C until the vegetables are tender and caramelised, tossing mid-way.
Add the tinned tomatoes, combine and cook for an additional 5 minutes.
Spoon the cooked vegetables onto your toast followed by the cheese.
Place on a baking tray and bake in the oven for 2-3 minutes or until the cheese has melted.
Add some fresh rocket before serving.

Herbed Onion and Parmesan

1/3 cups mayonnaise
1 cup shredded Parmesan cheese
1 cup finely sliced green onions
1 tablespoon chopped fresh dill
¼ teaspoon pepper
1 baguette/Ciabatta thinly sliced

Mix mayonnaise, Parmesan, green onions, dill and pepper.
Preheat your oven to grill.
Place you chosen bread on a baking sheet and grill until it starts to brown, about 1-2 minutes.
Turn slices over and spread Parmesan mixture generously on top.
Grill until topping is bubbly and starting to brown, 1 to 2 minutes.
Serve warm garnished with some added green onion.

Asparagus and Cheese Baguette

This is a great dish to serve to friends and family as a starter or with drinks.

2 tins white asparagus
(or green if white asparagus are not available)
100g grated Cheddar
(and Mozzarella for added creaminess)
2 tablespoons of mayonnaise
Salt and black pepper

Hollow out a baguette and fill with the mix of all ingredients.
Cook in a 200C oven for 10-15 minutes or until cheese is oozing and bread is crispy.
Other cheeses like Mozzarella or Gouda or a mix of all three can be used for some added indulgence and chopped spring onion can be added for a bit of zing!

Artichoke Hearts and Parmesan

My friend Karyn Moshal serves this dish regularly and as its one of my all-time favourites, I had to include it.

I tin of artichoke chopped hearts
½ cup mayonnaise
½ cup grated Parmesan cheese
A drop or two of Tabasco

Mix all ingredients together and pile into a small oven-proof container.
Cook for 30 -40 minutes at 190C until the top is browned, crisp and sizzling.
Serve with thin crisp slices of toast or toasted Pita.

Courgette, Pea and Cheese Omelette

2 eggs
1 thinly sliced onion
1 baby marrow, ribbons or thinly sliced batons
1 handful of peas
Grated Cheddar cheese
(or any other melty cheese)

Optional extras:
Tomatoes or red peppers are delicious in this dish too.

Fry the onions for 5-7 minutes in olive oil until soft.
Add the baby marrow and fry for a further few minutes until they become translucent.
Whisk the eggs and add them the cheese to the pan.
Fry until the egg is cooked and cheese is melted.
Add the peas at the last minute to maintain their colour.
Use frozen peas, thaw them in boiled water for 30 seconds.
Season with salt and pepper and
serve on buttered toast with watercress or a green salad.

Scrambled Egg with Shaved Bottarga

Bottarga is known as 'Mediterranean caviar'.
Bottarga can be thought of as the truffle of the sea, as it is commonly grated over dishes, just like the fungus, adding its unique aroma and flavour to many recipes.
This recipe is from Maureen Lipman and was a favourite of her late partner Guido Castro.

4 large eggs
2 teaspoons cup extra-virgin olive oil
2 tablespoon unsalted butter
1 tablespoon chopped parsley
1 tablespoon chopped chives
Thin baguette or Ciabatta is best for this
Finely shaved Bottarga or truffle
Salt and Freshly ground pepper

In a small bowl, whisk the eggs and the salt in a large non-stick skillet.
Heat the oil with 1 tablespoon of butter over very low heat.
Add the eggs and cook, stirring with a rubber spatula,
gradually adding the remaining butter, until soft and creamy.
Fold in the parsley and chives.
Toast the bread and shave or thinly slice the Bottarga.
Spoon the eggs onto the toasts and top with finely shaved Bottarga.
Season with salt and pepper.

Leeks and Cheese

When I was asking a few friends for their favourite indulgences, I knew Kim Issroff, one of my oldest friends would come up with something decadent and truly delicious. Here is her savoury suggestion, but check out her sweet option later in the book, it is truly spectacular! I had to keep this in her words, because even the recipe sounds indulgent.

There is something sublime about slow cooked leeks. But you have to take the time to cook them to make them lovely and smooth. And mix them with cheese and put them on toast and you have a healthy meal.

I like to cook them in butter and olive oil and I like mine finely sliced, the white and light green bits only, but you can adapt this recipe if you prefer bigger chunks or a bit of crunch. Choose whichever cheese works for you but make sure it is one that melts nicely – or use several cheeses if that is what is left over in your fridge

It's not fashionable, but I love a medium Cheddar rather than something strong as then I can still taste the leeks. Add your cheese/s and some single cream or milk to make a very thick sauce in your frying pan.

Preheat your grill Toast a couple of slices of bread – I like to use quite 'holey', airy bread rather than a dense, cakey one as the cheese oozes into the holes. Put your toast on a baking tray and put the sauce on the toast. Place under the grill until sizzling and oozing. Eat but watch out for burning your tongue as the cheese will be hot.

Pizza is essentially cheese on a toasted base loaded with delicious toppings. Here are some ways to use ready-made pizza dough, store bought pizza bases, toasted Pita, Naan or Flatbreads to make the perfect snack at home. For Tomato Sauce – use ready-made or there is a recipe for home-made sauce in the condiment section.

Buffalo Mozzarella, Olives and Fresh Rocket

Tomato Sauce
2 balls soft buffalo mozzarella
1 cup Kalamata olives
1 bag fresh rocket
Coarse salt and pepper
Good olive oil

Preheat your oven to 220 C.
Brush your base with olive oil and bake for about 5-7 minutes on a baking sheet until almost ready.
Remove from the oven and spoon on some tomato sauce and top with Mozzarella and halved olives.
Drizzle with olive oil.
Bake for a further 5 minutes or until the crusts are crisp and the cheese is melted and browned on top.
Season with salt and black pepper, drizzle with good olive oil and serve with fresh Rocket.

Mushrooms and Fresh Herbs

1½ cups sliced mixed mushrooms
(such as baby portabella, shiitake, and oyster)
1 tablespoon each finely chopped fresh thyme and Oregano
¼ teaspoon plus 1 pinch coarse salt, divided
1 tablespoon olive oil, plus more for drizzling
1 to 2 ounces goat cheese, crumbled
¾ cup shredded Mozzarella cheese
1 to 2 tablespoons finely chopped chives

Clean the mushrooms, pat dry and slice them.
In a sauté pan or skillet, heat 1 tablespoon olive oil to medium heat.
Add the mushrooms, chopped herbs, and salt and cook for about 5 minutes, stirring occasionally.
When mushrooms are tender, remove from the heat.
Prepare your base:
Preheat your oven to 220 C.
Brush your base with olive oil and bake for 5- 7 minutes on a baking sheet until almost ready.
Remove from the oven, spoon on tomato sauce and top with the Mozzarella cheese in an even layer.
Add the cooked mushrooms and crumbled goat cheese.
Bake until the cheese and crust are nicely browned.
Slice and serve immediately.

TRY SOME OF THESE PIZZA COMBINATIONS

Mozzarella is used most often for pizza, but try some other cheeses
like Cheddar, Gruyère or Parmesan

Prepare the base:
Either follow the instruction on ready-made pizza or pizza base.

If you are using mini Pita or flatbreads, brush with some olive oil and toast on a baking sheet in the oven at 200C for 5-7 minutes before adding your favourite toppings.

Remove from the oven, spoon on some tomato sauce and load with your favourite toppings and put back in the oven for a further 5 minutes or until the cheese has melted/

Mozzarella (other cheese), fresh tomato, fresh chilli and basil

Mozzarella, egg and spinach

Mozzarella, red peppers, olives, sundried tomato

Pesto, Mozzarella and thinly sliced fresh tomatoes, fresh red chilli (no tomato sauce)

Feta, marinated artichoke hearts, and Kalamata olives (no tomato sauce)

CHAPTER THREE

Loaded with Vegetables

Vegetables are essential (or so I've repeatedly told my nieces and nephews) and, allegedly, we need five a day at least. So I have included some easy and amazing ways to blend more veggies into your farinaceous (always wanted a chance to use that word) slices.

What could be better than a tasty meal that has only taken you a few minutes to prepare, but tastes and looks wonderful? This section combines every day ingredients, with a twist or two and gives you easy ways to elevate a couple of pieces of good bread and a few tangy vegetables and make them into a delicious snack for one or a popular meal for the whole family.

Fresh herbs are an invaluable addition to most dishes. They add flavour and colour. In most cases, using fresh instead of dried is best.

Fresh leaves such as watercress, Arugula, chives, basil and dill can be grown in a window box or in a patio and can transform a predictable dish into a taste sensation. Just try adding fresh accompaniments to any of the savoury dishes in this book, such as a handful of leaves, herbs or lettuce, or lobbing in some fresh lemon juice, olive oil, chillies and salt – and serving on the side with a spritz of black pepper. Mmmm … why do I find myself standing by the fridge again?

Beetroot and Burrata

Antipasti

Brie with Chutney

Caprese Toast

Fried Mushrooms

Mushroom Stroganoff

Tomato Bruschetta

Spanish Toast

Caramelized Red Onion

Tomato and Burrata

Marinated Aubergine

Grilled Aubergine

Falafel and Chopped Salad

Fresh Vegetables with
Green Goddess Dressing

Scrambled Egg with Bottarga

Fried Mashed Potato

White Bean Ragout

Humous

Baba Ghanoush

Butter Bean Pâté

Spicy Feta and Sundried Tomatoes

Slice and Assemble

You know those moments when you're standing in front of the fridge with no ideas on what to eat. These suggestions are for just those moments and can be put together using store-bought ingredients. I have given some bread suggestions, but any bread will do.

I have purposefully not given quantities, use as much or as little as you like! As a meal for one, I always have bagels or sliced sourdough in the freezer, so it easy to make a quick snack or meal. Or if you are looking for lunch ideas for the family, grab a fresh baguette or loaf of wholewheat from the supermarket and heap, cut in half, toast both sides under the grill in the oven (sprinkled with olive oil), heap with the ingredients and serve with a salad.

Beetroot and Burrata

Sliced beetroot

Burrata or Mozzarella

Watercress and extra-virgin olive oil

Brie with Chutney

Generous amount of Brie

Serve with chutney

Alternatively, put the toasted bread and Brie under grill for a minute or two, then serve with the chutney.

Antipasti

The flavours and colours make this an irresistible treat!

Artichoke Hearts in Olive Oil
Bottled Red peppers
Pesto and Mozzarella

Served with basil and a dash of olive oil.

Caprese Toast

Mozzarella
Tomatoes
Avocado

Spread the toast with Pesto
and layer with the rest of the ingredients.

Fried Mushrooms

1 punnet of button mushrooms
(portobello mushrooms would also work)

1 small onion

2 teaspoons fresh thyme leaves

2 tablespoons olive oil

Salt and ground black pepper

Gruyère cheese (optional)

Watercress or any fresh herbs for garnish

Finely slice the onion and fry in olive oil for about 6 minutes until they are soft and translucent.

Wash the mushrooms, pat dry and slice a medium thickness.

Add to the onions and fry for about 3 minutes, lower the heat if they begin to burn.

Sprinkle on a pinch of salt and a few turns of the pepper mill and the thyme leaves.

Toast 2 slices of your favourite bread and brush with olive oil.

Heap on the mushrooms.

Add grated Gruyère cheese and grill in the oven for a few minutes until the cheese has melted before serving with watercress or any other fresh herbs.

Mushroom Stroganoff

900g of mixed mushrooms
Cut into bite sized pieces
Use any varieties like button, wild, portobello
or assorted wild mushrooms
1 small onion
Salt and pepper
Dash of smoked Paprika
Chopped parsley or chives

Wash the mushrooms, pat dry and slice to a medium thickness.
Heat the oil in a frying pan and fry the sliced onions until they become translucent.
Add the mushrooms and fry for a further 2 minutes lowering the heat if they begin to burn.
Add a few tablespoons of cream or crème fraiche.
Season with Paprika, salt and pepper.
Serve garnished with chopped parsley or chives.

Tomato Bruschetta

4 large tomatoes, diced

4 tablespoons of extra-virgin olive oil

2 cloves garlic, thinly sliced

1 diced red onion

5 leaves thinly sliced basil

2 tablespoons of Balsamic vinegar

1 teaspoon of salt

Sliced baguette or Ciabatta

Extra-virgin olive oil for brushing

Fresh basil leaves for serving

In a large bowl toss together the tomatoes, onions, basil, vinegar, olive oil, salt and pepper.
Leave to marinate for 30 minutes.
Preheat oven to 200°C. Slice the baguette/Ciabatta and brush on both sides with olive oil and place on large baking tray.
Toast for about 10 minutes, turning halfway through, until golden.
After toasting, rub the bread on one side with halved garlic cloves.
Spoon the marinated tomato and onion mixture onto the bread just before serving and garnish with thinly sliced fresh basil.

Spanish Toast

This is a recipe my friend Pamela Norwitz learnt in Barcelona, the crisp toast almost melts the garlic and the tomatoes, which complement the crunchy coarse salt.
Very ripe tomatoes and a hearty, dense bread work best.

1 garlic clove, halved

2 small tomatoes, each cut in half crosswise, sweet/ripe tomatoes are best

1 teaspoon extra-virgin olive oil

Coarse salt and ground black pepper

Sourdough or Ciabatta work best

Place bread slices on grill rack.
Grill for 2 minutes on each side or until lightly browned.
Rub each slice of bread with garlic and tomato half (tomato pulp will rub off onto bread).
Discard tomato peels.
(If you prefer a bit more tomato, peel, deseed and pulp an extra tomato and spread on top).
Then drizzle with olive oil and sprinkle with salt and pepper.

Tomato and Burrata

3 tablespoons olive oil

1 clove garlic

1 punnet cherry tomatoes

1 ball burrata cheese

fresh basil

Coarse salt and freshly cracked black pepper

Sourdough, ciabatta or toast that will soak up the juices

Drizzle your toast with olive oil and rub with a garlic clove to infuse it with a little garlic flavour.
Marinate the tomatoes in olive oil, salt and pepper for a few minutes.
Slather the Burrata and tomatoes onto the toast and serve with some fresh basil.

Red Onion and Baby Tomato

50g butter

1 tablespoon olive oil

1 large red onion

300g packet of cherry tomatoes

1 clove of minced garlic

Several sprigs of thyme

Sliced Baguette or Ciabatta

Extra-virgin olive oil, for brushing

Heat the butter and oil in a frying pan until the butter has melted and fry the thinly sliced onion and minced garlic over a medium heat for about 10 minutes.
Tip the onion and juices into a bowl and set aside.
Preheat the oven to 200C.
Place the tomatoes on a baking tray and sprinkle generously with olive oil, salt and black pepper.
Roast for about 10-15 minutes, until the tomatoes are soft and just hold together.
Brush toasted bread with olive oil and layer on the onions and tomatoes.
Garnish with fresh thyme.

Marinated Aubergine

Or eggplant as it known in Australia.

As this recipe is a favourite of my sister-in-law Libby in Australia, I shall call it that in this recipe.

A delicious and handy veggie dish that keeps for a week!

Very yummy on any kind of toast and served with Labneh.

2 large eggplants, chopped into roughly 4cm x 2cm pieces

6 tablespoon extra virgin olive oil

½ tablespoon salt flakes plus a little extra

1½ tablespoon lemon juice

1 small garlic clove, crushed

Handful finely chopped parsley leaves

Preheat oven to 180C. Place eggplant in a large mixing bowl and drizzle with 2 tablespoons olive oil and a couple of pinches of salt flakes.

Toss well.

Place eggplant on a lined baking tray and bake until golden brown
(no need to turn over or throughout the baking), about 45 minutes.

While the eggplant is baking, make the marinade.

Use the same bowl (no need to dirty another!) and add in 4 tablespoons olive oil, the lemon juice, ½ teaspoon of salt flakes and garlic and gently whisk to combine.

When the eggplant is ready, remove from oven, allow to cool for a few minutes and transfer into the bowl with the marinade.

Gently mix (so as not to mush the eggplant) and sprinkle with parsley.

Serve at room temperature.

Keep any leftovers in an air tight glass container in the fridge for up to a week.

Grilled Aubergine with Tomato and Mozzarella

1 large aubergine
Olive oil
Coarse salt and pepper
Tomato and Mozzarella
Pesto or Tahini dressing (optional)

Cut aubergine lengthways into 5mm thick slices and place in single layer on a baking tray lined with greaseproof paper.
Brush both sides generously with olive oil and sprinkle with salt.
Bake at 180C until soft and beautifully golden, about 10 minutes each side.
On your chosen Toast (or in mini Pita), layer the cooked aubergines with sliced tomatoes and Mozzarella.
Season with salt, black pepper and olive oil.
Pesto or Tahini dressing go brilliantly with this dish.

Falafel and Chopped Salad

Home-Made Baked Falafel

¼ cup + 1 tablespoon extra-virgin olive oil

1 tin chickpeas, remove the liquid and dry well

½ cup roughly chopped red onion

½ cup packed fresh parsley

¼ cup packed fresh coriander

4 cloves garlic, quartered

1 teaspoon salt and pepper

½ teaspoon ground cumin

¼ teaspoon ground cinnamon

Preheat oven to 180C.

Pour ¼ cup of the olive oil into a large, rimmed baking sheet and spread until the pan is evenly coated.

In a food processor, combine the chickpeas, onion, parsley, coriander, garlic, salt, pepper, cumin, cinnamon, and the remaining 1 tablespoon of olive oil.

Process until smooth, about 1 minute.

Using your hands, scoop out about 2 tablespoons of the mixture at a time.

(Makes 12 Falafel balls)

Shape the Falafel into small patties.

Place the falafel on your heated oiled pan.

Bake for 25-30 minutes, carefully flipping the Falafels halfway through baking, until they are deeply golden on both sides.

Allow to cool before assembling.

You can also use a packet of Falafel mix or ready-made Falafel balls, both available at most supermarkets.

Chopped Salad

3 diced tomatoes

3 diced Israeli cucumbers

1 small diced onion

1 teaspoon of chopped dill

Add 3 tablespoons of olive oil and the juice of 1 small lemon to the diced salad and season with salt and black pepper.

Serve the Falafel and salad on toasted Pita or flatbreads with Tahini sauce.

Make sure to have some extra sauce available for dipping, it's delicious and messy.

Peas, Carrots, Radishes and Sprouts with a Green Goddess Dressing

For the dressing:

1 clove garlic, grated

½ onion, roughly chopped

Zest of ½ lemon and juice of 1 lemon

¾ cup mayonnaise

¾ cup whole milk Greek yogurt

¾ cup packed freshly chopped parsley leaves

¼ cup packed freshly chopped mint leaves

¼ cup packed freshly chopped basil

2 green onions, thinly sliced

2 tablespoon freshly chopped chives

1½ teaspoons coarse salt

½ teaspoon ground black pepper

To make the dressing, blend all ingredients until smooth
The dressing can be refrigerated in an airtight container for up to 1 week.

To assemble:

Combine ½ a cup of frozen peas
(boil the kettle and pour over peas and leave for 30 seconds),
finely sliced radishes, Juliennes or finely diced carrots, and a handful of sprouts
(or use any of your favourite raw vegetables like avocado, cucumbers, tomatoes or peppers).

Toast your chosen bread, brush with olive oil.

Generously spoon on the Green Goddess dressing and layer your vegetables.

Sprinkle with pumpkin seeds for some added crunch or add sliced chicken
or flaked salmon if you want some added protein.

Fried Mashed Potato on Toast

Ok, so this sounds weird, and it is not healthy, but you simply have to try it's delicious.

This is a recipe from my friend Matthew (see his masterclass on French Toast on page 00).

It's best to use left over mashed potato for this recipe (from cold works fine).

Matthew's mom used to deliberately make loads of mashed potato for dinner to ensure there was enough for frying for a delicious after-school lunch.

Per person you'll need about a cup of mashed potato

2 teaspoons of butter and a bit of olive oil

In a non-stick pan melt the butter and add the oil.

When hot, put in the mashed potato flatten out, letting it colour underneath.

Mix up the potato and keep on frying until the whole mixture starts to turn golden with brown flecks.

You need to take your time and not rush, mixing as you go and adding a bit more butter or oil if the mixture becomes too dry.

Once nicely coloured, season well especially with a good grinding of black pepper and place a good dollop on your favourite slice of toast.

This works really well with a nutty flavoured seed load but any toast can work.

Eat it plain (with more pepper) or add crispy bits of bacon or sliced fresh tomato or whatever else you fancy.

(I have refrained from using bacon throughout this book, because although this is not a kosher book, I am Jewish and as such bacon is a no-no. However, Matthew has included bacon in both his recipe, so I have decided to leave it in as an option for those who would like to use it.)

White Bean Ragout

1 medium onion, chopped
2 tablespoons extra-virgin olive oil plus
Coarse salt, freshly ground pepper
2 garlic cloves (1 finely grated, 1 halved)
1 teaspoon tomato paste
1 tin white/butter beans, rinsed and drained
1 tin chopped tomato
2 slices grilled or toasted Ciabatta (or your favourite toast)
4 tablespoons finely grated Parmesan (optional)
Chopped flat-leaf parsley

Heat olive oil over a medium heat.
Fry finely chopped onion and garlic until soft, but not brown.
Add beans and tinned tomatoes and simmer for a further 2 minutes.
Add tomato paste and season with salt and pepper and simmer for a few more minutes.
Brush 2 slices of toast with olive oil and sprinkle with ½ the Parmesan.
In a pre-heated oven at 200C, bake for about 5 minutes, or until the bread is toasted and the cheese is just starting to brown.
Top the toast with the hot bean mixture and sprinkle over the rest of the Parmesan and return to the oven for a few minutes until the cheese has melted.
Garnish with parsley and drizzle with olive oil.

Here are some easy and totally delicious dips that work brilliantly served with toasted pita or any thinly toasted bread

Humous

1 tin drained chickpeas

4 tablespoons tahini paste

2 minced garlic cloves

Juice of 1 lemon

Salt, pepper and olive oil

Drain and mash the chickpeas with a fork or masher
(or puree in a food processor if you prefer a smoother texture).

Add the Tahini paste, minced garlic and lemon juice and mix together
(add bit of water if it's too thick).

Season with salt and pepper.

Serve with a glug of olive oil on top.

Baba Ghanoush

1 large aubergine

3 minced garlic cloves

4 teaspoons of tahini paste

Olive oil

Cut the aubergine in half and sprinkle with salt
and brush with 2 teaspoons of olive oil.

Bake in a medium oven at 200C for about 30 minutes, until mashable.

Spoon out the insides, discarding the skins.

Place in a small bowl and mix in the garlic and Tahini.

Season with salt and pepper and serve with a glug of olive oil on top.

Butter Bean Pâté

1 tin butter beans, drained and rinsed
1 small garlic clove, roughly chopped
1-2 tablespoons lemon juice
2 tablespoons Greek-style yogurt

Blitz the butter beans, garlic, lemon juice and the yogurt in a blender until smooth.
Season with salt and pepper.
Add a splash more lemon juice if needed.
Serve with a glug of olive oil.

Spicy Feta and Sundried Tomatoes

This is another favourite courtesy of Karyn Moshal.

100g Philadelphia cream cheese
100g feta cheese
½ a finely chopped red chilli
3 sundried tomatoes in oil
and one spoon of the oil from the jar

Blend all the ingredients in a mixer.
Refrigerate for at least an hour to allow flavours to blend.

Spinach and Sour Cream

This is a truly spectacular dish, that is certainly not for those trying to watch the calories, but works as a quick and delicious centrepiece to impress friends.

Especially if you need something impressive when friends come round for a drink.

This recipe was given to me by my friend Pamela Norwitz and exactly what I would expect to get when visiting.

2 cup frozen chopped spinach

1 cup mayonnaise

1 container sour cream

1 teaspoon salt

¼ teaspoon pepper

1 packet vegetable or onion soup mix

Thaw the spinach and drain.

Put in a sieve and squeeze dry to remove excess liquid.

In a large bowl, stir together the chopped spinach, mayonnaise, sour cream, salt, pepper and soup mix.

Cover and refrigerate for at least 1 hour.

Serve in a 'Bread Bowl': Slice the top off a round loaf of bread (sourdough works best here).

Hollow out the bread.

Toast the inside in the oven sprinkled liberally with olive oil to make croutons for dipping.

And serve with additional slices of toasted sourdough or baguette slices.

CHAPTER FOUR

Add Some Protein

Adding some meat, chicken or fish are excellent ways to turn a toasted sandwich into a balanced meal. Once again simple recipes are best. Most proteins need cooking, so here are some great easy ways to transmogrify it
(always wanted to use that word too!) on to toast.

Tinned sardines
Tuna with lettuce and fresh dill
Smoked salmon and poached eggs
Rare roast beef
Chicken livers and onion
Chicken liver pâtè
Greek style chicken
Turkey patties
Schnitzel and horseradish cream
Grilled steak with Chimichurri
Prego roll

SLICE AND ASSEMBLE

Sardines, Onion and Tomato

Drain a tin of sardines
Butter or Olive oil your toast
Layer sardines then thinly sliced sweet onion and tomatoes
Add a splash of lemon juice and olive oil Season with black pepper

Smoked Salmon and Boiled Egg

Smoked Salmon
Avocado
Poached or boiled egg

Seasoned with salt and pepper.
Garnished with rocket.

Tuna and Fresh Dill

Tin of tuna
Finely shredded iceberg lettuce
Handful of chopped dill
Olive Oil, Red wine vinegar and salt

Combine all ingredients and crumble over some Feta to serve.

Rare Roast Beef

Thinly sliced roast beef
(or any other cold meat)

Spread your toast with mustard and mayonnaise.
Serve with tomato and pickled cucumber.

Chicken Liver Pâtè

3 tablespoons olive oil
1 pound chicken livers
3 cloves garlic
1 onion, chopped
1 sprig of rosemary
1 sprig of thyme
1 teaspoon salt
1 teaspoon pepper
3 tablespoons melted butter for topping (optional)

Finely chop the onions and garlic and fry in oil until tender and translucent.
Wash the chicken livers and get rid of any fat.
Cut them to half and pat dry with kitchen paper.
Add the livers to the frying onions and cook at a medium heat for 4-6 minutes.
Add the rosemary, thyme, salt and pepper and sauté for another few minutes.
Put the ingredients in a food processor and blend until smooth.
Spread liver pâtè into a dish and top with melted butter (iptional).
Chill in the fridge for 1-2 hours.
Serve with toasted Pita or any thin slices of toast.

Chicken Livers and Onions

500g chicken livers (one packet for 2 people)
4 tablespoon sunflower oil
2 medium onions
2 tablespoons of tomato ketchup
1 tablespoon marjoram
1 tablespoon thyme
½ teaspoon black pepper
2 pinches of salt

Cut the onions in half and thinly slice..
Fry in vegetable oil until tender and translucent.
Wash the chicken livers and get rid of any fat.
Cut them to half and pat dry with kitchen paper.
Add the livers to the frying onions and cook at a high heat for 4 minutes.
Don't overcook the livers, they become hard.
Add the ketchup and season with black pepper, salt, marjoram and thyme.
Cook for another few minutes.
When the livers are soft and ready, spoon generously over toast and garnish with watercress.
Best served with crunchy toast like sourdough, baguette or Ciabatta.

Greek Style Chicken

2 flattened chicken breasts
Marinade: 2 tablespoons of olive oil
¼ teaspoon dried oregano
Juice of ½ a lemon
Salt and pepper

Serve with a Chopped Salad
2 tomatoes, finely diced
1 cucumber, finely diced
¼ red onion, finely diced

Dress the salad with Juice of ½ a lemon.
2 tablespoons olive oil
Salt and pepper and a sprinkling of dried Oregano

Or a Quick Slaw
3 tablespoons apple or white balsamic vinegar
1 tablespoon of olive oil
½ teaspoon salt and black pepper
½ teaspoon chopped dill
½ cabbage (red, white or both)
½ teaspoon caraway seeds (optional)

Finely slice the cabbage and dill and put in a mixing bowl.
Add all other ingredients and toss well to coat.
Cover and chill until ready to serve.

Optional:
Add a tablespoon of mayonnaise to make it a bit creamier.
Heat a griddle pan until very hot and flash fry the chicken breast so you can see and smell the char marks.
Cut the charred chicken into strips and assemble with the salad into a toasted flatbread.
For a family meal, make double the quantity and serve in a toasted loaf.

Turkey Burgers

These can also be made using minced beef, chicken or lamb, but freshly made patties, served burger style on a toasted bun, loaded with salad is delicious.

450g turkey mince

1 tablespoon onion, finely chopped

1 teaspoon chopped parsley

½ teaspoon salt

1 tablespoon olive oil

¼ teaspoon cayenne pepper

½ teaspoon chili pepper flakes, optional

2 teaspoon minced garlic

Combine all ingredients (ground turkey, onion, parsley, garlic, salt, cayenne, ginger, and chili flakes) in a medium-sized bowl.

Then divide the turkey mixture into four equal parts and flatten gently to form the turkey patties.

Heat 1 tablespoon oil in a skillet over medium-high heat and sear the patties for 5-8 minutes, flip over and sear on the other side.

Make sure to give a good sear to the turkey patties so they're crispy on the outside and soft on the inside.

Serve on a toasted bun with mayonnaise, mustard, pickles, lettuce, cucumber, pickled cabbage (or as many or as few of these as you prefer).

For a family meal, place on the buns and lay out the accompaniments for everyone to help themselves

Schnitzel and Horseradish

2 boneless, skinless chicken breasts
Coarse salt and Freshly ground black pepper
1 large eggs, beaten
¼ cup all-purpose flour
1 cup of breadcrumbs or panko breadcrumbs

Cut each chicken breast lengthwise until you have two thin halves of chicken breast.
Place one breast in a large plastic bag or under plastic wrap, and pound with a rolling pin.
Season with salt and pepper.
Fill a large saucepan with about ¼-inch of oil and heat.
Set up one plate of each of the three breading ingredients: flour, eggs, and breadcrumbs.
Place one breast into the flour and flip, covering with flour, then move to the egg and do the same.
Finally, place into the breadcrumbs to coat, but do not press breadcrumbs into the meat.
Carefully drop the breasts into your oil and fry 2-3 minutes on both sides or until the cutlet is crispy and golden brown.
Move to a paper towel lined plate and immediately season with coarse salt.

Horseradish Cream

½ cup crème fraiche
1 to 2 tablespoons horseradish
(freshly grated or jarred horseradish)
1 pinch salt
1 pinch black pepper

In a small bowl, mix together crème fraiche and horseradish.
Start off by adding 1 tablespoon horseradish.
Mix everything together and taste, adding more horseradish for more kick.
Add salt and pepper to taste.
Served on crusty toast or a toasted flatbread with roasted baby vine tomatoes.

Grilled Steak with Chimichurri

This recipe works best with any kind of crusty white toast.

Marinade for the steak

2/3 cup olive oil

½ cup fresh orange juice

¼ cup fresh lime juice

¼ cup soy sauce

¼ cup Worcestershire sauce

3 tablespoons apple cider or red wine vinegar

4 garlic cloves minced

2 x 1cm thick fillet steaks

Salt and pepper to taste

For the Chimichurri Sauce

1 cup fresh parsley

1 cup fresh cilantro

¼ cup olive oil

½ medium onion diced

3 garlic cloves

3 tablespoons fresh lime juice

2 tablespoons red wine vinegar

½ teaspoon salt

½ teaspoon pepper

For the marinade:
Whisk all of the ingredients together and marinade the steak for about 30 minutes.
When the steaks are ready, season with salt and pepper.
Heat the griddle pan to a high heat and fry for 3-4 minutes turning midway.
Remove from the heat and allow to rest.

For the Chimichurri:
Blend all the ingredients in a food processor until everything is chopped up and smooth.
Slice the rested steak into 2 cm thickness and serve with a liberal serving of the Chimichurri.
Best served with crunchy toast to soak up all the sauce.

Prego Roll

This is classic South African dish that has its roots in Portugal.

2 x 1cm thick fillet steaks

1 bay leaves

1 cloves of garlic finely chopped

¼ bottle white wine

2 whole peppercorns

1 tablespoon Peri-Peri sauce/ Harissa or hot sauce
(Nando's make the best Peri-Peri sauce ever!
It's available at most large supermarkets)

½ teaspoon cumin

Coarse salt and black pepper

¼ cup olive oil

Portuguese bread rolls

To prepare the steak:
Place the steaks on a board and top with the chopped garlic clove.
Cover with some plastic wrap and hammer them with a mallet until they are about a ½ inch thick.
Season with coarse salt.

For the marinade:
In a bowl combine the white wine, bay leaves, peppercorns, peri-peri and cumin.
Whisk together to combine.
Add the steaks and marinade steaks for a few hours or overnight.
Remove the steaks from the refrigerator 2 hours before cooking to bring them to room temperature.

To cook the steaks:
Heat a grill pan on high.
Add olive oil.
Remove steaks from the marinade and pat them dry.
Cook for 2-3 minutes a side depending on desired level of doneness.
Set aside to rest and then slice.
Add the remaining marinade to the grill pan and reduce by half so it forms a thick sauce.
Add the steak back to the pan to coat.
Layer the steak onto the toast and pour over the pan juice.
Serve with tomato and cucumber and some Peri-Peri sauce on the side.

Loafing

By Maureen Lipman

I'm not hungry, why should I be?
I've just had yoghurt and ginseng tea.
I've gargled mouthwash, checked what's app,
Recycled the chateau neuf du pape,
But oddly, the thing I'm wanting most,

Is a doorstep slice of buttered toast?

I've downward dog'd and bleached my teeth,
Had a freezing walk on a friendless heath,
Ground my teeth at predictive text.
Wondered, out loud, what the hell comes next.
Considered the dinner I'd like to host

While longing for cheese on sourdough toast

I've put out seeds for the mother bird
Whilst pondering marmite or lemon curd?
Inhaled while sniffing 'first defence'
And checked the fate of poor Mike Pence.

I've thought about moving to the coast
But meanwhile, I'd die for a piece of toast.

Buttered toast with marmalade
Chopped boiled eggs, freshly laid
Spurs on three with Gary Lineker?
Smashed sardines black pepper and vinegar

Dover sole in foil for Sunday roast,
Lord, I'd sell my soul for a slice of toast.

CHAPTER FIVE

Sweet Things

Let's face it, Nutella on French Toast Recipe will make some folks gag and others jump out of bed in the morning! Is it a decadent, indulgent breakfast treat or an impeccable treat?

There are many ways to make a piece of toast into a delicious sweet sensation. You could add chargrilled peaches or grilled bananas or jazz up your favourite jam and splash it on all over.

Here are some real sweethearts to counter-balance all the savouries! In this section there are some opportunities to use sweet options too and make some mouth-watering breakfasts, brunch or snacks. As an alternative bread, you could try using Brioche, Challah or Panettoni to make something extra indulgent.

What is French Toast?

It is alternatively known as Gypsy toast (mind the cultural appropriation abyss), Nun's toast or Poor Knights of Windsor toast? It seems to have been created by Joseph French the dish in 1724, who advertised it as 'French Toast'.
He meant to write French's Toast but, perhaps anticipating Twentieth Century grammar, or lack of it, he forgot the apostrophe.

The French call it Pain Perdu (meaning 'lost bread') and the Italians call it Pan Dulcis. Whatever the name, the dish typically starts with stale bread, soaked in an egg and milk custard, then fried in butter, then topped with an array of sins like extra butter (good cholesterol it seems now, after all those wretched years of *marge*), maple syrup, berries, bananas, Pistachio or almond butter or sweetened whipped cream.

Chargrilled Peaches with Labneh
Figs with Goats Cheese
Labneh and Cherry Jam
Banana and Peanut Butter
French Toast
Strawberries and Mascarpone
Apples and Cinnamon
Nutella and Strawberries
Grilled Banana and Peanut Butter
Ricotta and Pistachio
Sweet Tahini and Halva
Banana and Peanut Butter
Banana Bread
Panettone with Chocolate

Slice and Assemble

Quick Options using fruit.

Brioche is an obvious choice for sweet options, but most toast works just as well.

These are Oh so simple, but truly delicious!

Chargrilled Peaches with Labneh

Chargrill fresh or tinned peaches in a little oil or butter for 1-2 minute until lightly charred.

Spread the Labneh on your toast and add the fruit.

Garnish with mint and dust with icing sugar.

Use any stone fruit such as apricots or plums.

Figs with Goat's Cheese

1 log of Goat's cheese
(it's sometimes labelled as chevre cheese)

Fresh figs or figs in syrup

Honey to taste

Bring goat's cheese to room temperature (about an hour) and whip in a bowl until silky smooth.

Spread the cheese on your toast and layer with sliced figs.

Drizzle honey and add some nuts for crunch.

Labneh and Cherry Jam with Pine Nuts

Spread Labneh on toast.
Use cherry jam and some tinned cherries
for extra fruitiness.
Garnish with pine nuts.

Cream Cheese and Apricots

This is another Karyn Moshal favourite.

Tinned or poached apricots
Or any fruit such as poached peaches or plums
100g Philadelphia/soft cream cheese
1 tablespoon lemon curd or half a spoon lemon juice
1 tablespoon icing sugar

Mix the cheese together with the lemon curd or lemon juice.
Sweeten with icing sugar to taste.
Spread on toasted Brioche.
Top with the fruit.

French Toast

This is a masterclass in how to make the ultimate French Toast. One of my most favourite people, Matthew Van Lierop, is one of my friends who can make the simplest ingredients look and taste spectacular. Here is his recipe for French Toast. I have left it in his words, because I simply had to!

There are lots of recipes for French Toast/Pain Perdu. My approach has always been to make it worth it or not have it at all, so for 2 people, take 3 lovely eggs, 3 teaspoons of heavy cream and give it a good whisk.

Using day old bread (stale but not dry) cut some fat slices. The best is a lovely French baguette cut at a jaunty 45deg angle into thick slices. Dunk the slices in the egg mixture and let this all get sucked up – work on two or three slices per person. This is where you need to be patient to let the bread soak up the egg. French toast with 'bread' in the middle is a no-no.

Heat a large frying pan and add 4 teaspoons or more of unsalted butter, let this sizzle but not get brown and add the bread slices. Let it brown nicely and then flip and do the other side. You want to have a low heat and cook for a longer time, making sure the French toast has a bit of colour but is also cooked through properly. Once cooked, drain on some kitchen towel for a few moments and then serve.

Strawberries and Mascarpone

Toss the strawberries in some sugar.

Serve with a good dollop of Mascarpone or sweetened Ricotta (and syrup if you like).

Serve with some extra strawberries dipped in chocolate (white or dark) for some extra indulgence.

Nutella and Strawberries

While your toast is still warm, spread generously with Nutella and top with fresh strawberries.

Serve with some extra strawberries dipped in chocolate (white or dark) for some extra indulgence.

Apples and Cinnamon

Tinned pie apples with 2 teaspoons of castor sugar and ½ a teaspoon of cinnamon.

Or peel, core and slice an apple into a saucepan, add 3 tablespoons water and gently until the apples are soft, add caster sugar and cinnamon. Serve with maple syrup.

Grilled Banana and Peanut Butter

2 tablespoon brown sugar

1 large banana, halved lengthwise

2 tablespoons peanut butter

Place brown sugar on a plate; dip cut sides of banana in sugar. Place banana cut side up on a baking sheet; grill for 3-5 minutes, rotating often, until banana is browned. Spread the toast with peanut butter and top with the roasted banana.

Ricotta and Pistachio

2 tablespoons light Ricotta cheese
1 slice crusty whole-grain toast
1 teaspoon olive oil
1 tablespoon crushed dry-roasted salted pistachios

Spread Ricotta cheese on crusty whole-grain toas.
Drizzle olive oil over Ricotta and sprinkle with Pistachios.

Sweet Tahini and Halva

¼ cup tahini paste
2 tablespoons honey
1 tablespoon water
¼ teaspoon cinnamon
½ teaspoon vanilla (optional)

Mix together Tahini paste, honey, water and vanilla.
Spread over your toast and sprinkle with sesame seeds and crumbled Halva.

Peter's Banana and Peanut Butter

Spread peanut butter on two pieces of bread.
Top with thinly slice banana
Toast in a Panini press or sandwich maker.
Or simply spread peanut butter on your favourite toast and top with sliced banana.

Gluten free Banana Bread

This is the only recipe where I have included the making of the bread. I have done this because toasted banana bread is one of my favourite things and it is not always easy to find ready-made. And this is a healthy treat, which is exactly what I would have expected from my lovely sister-in-law Hayley in South Africa, who sent me this recipe

This recipe is a one bowl wonder! No mixer required for this super moist, easy gluten-free banana bread. Has a dairy-free option too

2 to 3 very ripe bananas mashed

1/3 cup melted unsalted butter (can use coconut oil to make it dairy-free)

1 teaspoon bicarb of soda

1½ cups gluten-free flour

1/4 teaspoon Xanthan gum (leave out if it's already in your flour)

Pinch of salt

¾ cup granulated sugar (½ cup if you like it less sweet)

2 large eggs beaten

1 teaspoon pure vanilla extract

Preheat the oven to 180 degrees C. Spray a loaf tin with cooking spray.

In a mixing bowl, mash the ripe banana until smooth. Add the bicarb of soda to the mashed bananas.

Stir the melted butter into the mashed bananas then stir in the sugar, salt, beaten eggs and pure vanilla extract.

Mix in the gluten-free flour and Xanthan gum (unless it's already included in your flour).

Pour the batter into the greased loaf tin and bake on the centre rack for 50 mins to 1 hour or until a toothpick inserted in the centre, comes out clean.

Cool completely before slicing.

Store in an air-tight container and pop into the toaster whenever you feel like a taste of heaven.

Enjoy!!

* You may experience different baking results depending on the gluten-free blend you choose.
* The best way to measure gluten-free flour is the "level spoon" method. Once you've scooped the flour into the measuring cup, use the back of a knife or spoon to level off the top of the cup.
* Three mashed bananas are equal to 1 cup.
* Dairy free options: any dairy-free butter or coconut oil can be used
* Can always add mini chocolate chips, blueberries, nuts and/or raisins for more yumminess.
* Always bake with ingredients that are at room temperature. Ingredients at different temperatures tend to not mix well.

This is delicious served toasted with butter or for something extra indulgence, serve with maple syrup, banana slices, chopped walnuts and garnished with whipped cream or crème fraiche.

Panettone with Chocolate

Another of Kim's decadent and delicious dishes. I had to keep it in her words, because the way she describes the process sounds almost as good as the result tastes. It is not always easy to get Panettone, so use a fruit loaf as an alternative, it tastes just a good!

This one is best made for only 1 or 2 people as it's messy and should be eaten soon after cooking. If you have some leftover panettone (or let's be honest, it's worth buying some for this pudding/breakfast/brunch/lunch, cut 2 slices per person, fairly thick – you want it crispy on the outside and soft on the inside.

Toast on both sides – I find this easiest on a non-stick frying pan but can be done under the grill or on a flat griddle pan – be careful as it burns easily. Butter one side of each piece of toast and grate some chocolate – any chocolate will do – whatever you prefer – though white might be cloying.

Melt some butter in your frying pan (you could add some olive oil too but this is not a low-calorie recipe) and put your first slice in butter side down and sprinkle on as much chocolate as you like. Put second slice on top, butter side up and when you're ready, turn it so that the butter is on the bottom and the toast cooks a bit more in the butter. By now, your chocolate should be melting and perhaps oozing a bit.

Remove from the frying pan and pimp it a bit.

You might want cream or ice cream, or crème fraiche.

Or if fruit and chocolate is your thing, fresh berries would work well to cut through some the richness or you might want to make a little sauce of raspberries which you've simply heated with some icing sugar and lemon juice. Some sprigs of mint always make things looks pretty.
(Although do look out for the type of panettone – some already have chocolate in and others have lots of candied fruit so adding more fruit may be overwhelming.)

THE LAST SLICE IN THE RACK

Maureen Lipman

Something about this book prompted a deeply buried of memory of childhood:

'Mam, can we have one of them things for tea?'

'Well … you'll have to do it over the gas, because I'm not drawing a fire.'

Now this was the early 1950's and what's more the 1950s in suburban Hull, so the choice of what you had for tea was limited to beans on toast, eggs on toast, tinned spaghetti hoops on – yes you guessed it, grilled Wonderloaf. This was in the days before Cap'n Birdseye launched a thousand chips and fish fingers. Weekday 'tea' was always one of the afore mentioned delicacies before Dad came home and had a proper man's dinner, newspaper propped up in front of his nose, at six thirty.

Breakfast was cereal on the run, lunch at school was Mince, Mash and Fly cemetery – don't ask… Well ok – I don't want you phoning Child-line on my behalf – it was a dusty shortcrust pie with even dustier raisins secreted inside it.

So, imagine our glee when Mam produced one day, this incredible new gadget and drew a fire in the grate. My brother and I stopped rowing for long enough to take turns holding 'One of them things' over the flame until it was browned.

'Don't sit too near! Kids! Sit further back, you might go up.'

My brother would have Kraft cheese slices in his 'thing', and I would have banana or beans. The gadget consisted of two long handles which opened up a space ship shaped disc into which you placed your bread and filling. The non-circular corners of the bread were cut off by the edge of the discs and fed, post haste, to the sparrows. When it was toasted on both sides, which took long enough for Geoffrey and I to start another row, it was dropped onto your plate and then the sheer ha..ha..ha hotness of it meant another longish wait before biting into the actual, toasted, delicious, runny sandwich. Then there was tinned fruit and packet jelly to follow. And a sigh of relief from the chef … Job done. Afterwards, we raced back outside, to join our motley crew of mates, back into the 'ten-foot' between the backs of the houses for more double ball against the wall. I don't know why we weren't fat and unhealthy but we weren't. Vegetables? My mother could put the vegetables on at the same time as she put the chicken in to roast. Until I came to London, aged nineteen, I actually thought sprouts and cabbage were bright yellow with the texture of a noodle.

Bananas or beans reminds me of the currently trending discussion about whether one can eat Weetabix with baked beans. Automatic upchuck right? I heard Jacob Rees-Mogg wade in to the debate with his own brand of posh 'eurgh'.

'Well, sounds ghastly to me,' he groaned. 'Weetabix are ghastly, baked beans are ghastly. Besides, you know what I have for breakfast. Nanny's homemade marmalade on toast!' We must send him a copy of *This Book is Toast*.

Nowadays, Wonderloaf and Mother's Pride are regarded with the same suspicion as Benson and Hedges and people take wonder and pride in having their own 'mothers'. Meaning their own living yeasts which they nurse lovingly and store in secret, yeasty places to be used and reused at will. Bread making machines turn out Ciabatta and Sourdough of a morning and the range of breads in the supermarkets and artisan bread shops is confounding. Gluten-free for the true coeliac and the uber-intolerants, seeded, flat breads, wraps, Pitta, Polish rye, Charcoal, Challah, poppy seed Challah – even marzipan Challah, lord help me. People walk around eating baguettes the size of a human leg, dripping with lettuce and turkey and Quinoa and gherkins and capers and Mozzarella and hot pepper sauce, and an egg!

This is not my thing. My thing is that bread, and specifically toasted bread, is my absolute and special treat. In the same way I wouldn't want a coffee machine in my home … so George Clooney if you were thinking of dropping off your old Nespresso Citiz on my birthday, thanks but no thanks. I want to go out for my coffee. It doesn't have to be GREAT coffee, although that helps, it just has to be my reward for a good long walk or a piece of work finished … well, what else is there, with which you can earn your coffee, in these lockdown, schloch-down days?

My Desert Island starter? Parmesan toast with anchovy custard, since you ask.

Or pretty well most of the recipes in this joyous, toasty 'hygge' book.

I normally have a joke for every subject at the ready just in case a speech is required on the hop.

But for toast? This is the nearest I can do for you

Toastmaster joke

A toastmaster has an important dinner that evening. He goes to pick up his black trousers but finds the dry cleaner has closed for the day. He tries on his spare pair but they split down the middle when he bends over. He rushes round to the little Yiddishe tailor in Soho who agrees to drop everything and make him a pair of trousers from scratch. The toastmaster goes to pick them up on his way to the dinner and is so delighted with them that he not only pays him but gives him a spare ticket for the swanky dinner at the Dorchester.

Later that night the Toastmaster is ushering the guests into the magnificent ballroom:

'Colonel and Mrs. Ledbury Smythe,' he bellows to the room at large.

'Brigadier and Lady Fawcett DcM PQK.'

'Sir Bingham Deveraux M.P. and the Honourable Jemima-Creighton Sidings.'

Suddenly a tubby little old man appears at the entrance door'

The toastmaster leans down and asks him for his name.

'Er … it's me, Sam,' he whispers back, nervously.

'What's that?' rasps the toastmaster, eager to get on …

'It's me, Sam…' repeats the embarrassed tailor.

'Sam? Sam what pray…' the toastmaster is getting impatient now.

'I made your trousers!' explains Sam.

The toastmaster pushes him forward and bellows to the room:

'MAJOR TROUSERS!'

THE LAST WORD

Heidi Nathan

As a first timer in the realm of putting a book together, I didn't realise how much was really involved. So I have to thank the people who have made this idea into a reality. This book may have come about during COVID 19, but in actual fact, when lockdown is a distant memory, these recipes will still stand the test of time. If toast was indeed invented as a delicacy for the Pharaohs, we can all agree it will be a delicacy for a long time coming?

Of course, I need to start with my dearest friend Maureen Lipman, who without her huge shove this would never have happened. What started as a throw-away comment on a walk in the park is now a book. Her collaboration has been invaluable and I don't know how to say thank you enough.

David Cohen, my publisher – who took on a real novice and with such patience has made this into an actual book. (I still can't believe I have a book published.)

My family are always my biggest cheerleaders and are behind me in everything I do, so thank you United Nathans for your unconditional love and support.

Then of course there are my friends and family who contributed recipes. These are some of my nearest and dearest who are food-lovers like me who offered recipes to be included. My sisters-in-law Hayley and Libby, and friends Pamela Norwitz, Karyn Moshal, Kim Issroff, and Matthew van Lierop.

Thank you, too, Karol Gladki, chef and food stylist and Maria Andrews, photographer, who have successfully helped make sure that every piece of toast looks delicious.

A toast to everyone as we hopefully soon emerge bleary eyed from this strangest of years.